GROW YOUR MIND

MAKE MISTAKES

Written by Izzi Howell
Illustrated by David Broadbent

W
FRANKLIN WATTS
LONDON • SYDNEY

Franklin Watts
First published in Great Britain in 2019 by The Watts Publishing Group
Copyright © The Watts Publishing Group, 2019

Produced for Franklin Watts by
White-Thomson Publishing Ltd
www.wtpub.co.uk

Izzi Howell has asserted her right to be identified as the author of this
Work in accordance with the Copyright, Designs and Patents Act 1988.

Series Designer: David Broadbent
All Illustrations by: David Broadbent

Every attempt has been made to clear copyright. Should there be any
inadvertent omission please apply to the publisher for rectification.

Printed in China

Franklin Watts
An imprint of
Hachette Children's Group
Part of The Watts Publishing Group
Carmelite House
50 Victoria Embankment
London EC4Y 0DZ

An Hachette UK Company
www.hachette.co.uk
www.franklinwatts.co.uk

Facts, figures and dates were correct when going to press.

CONTENTS

Mistakes and mindsets

When was the last time you made a mistake? It probably wasn't too long ago as everyone **makes mistakes** every day. It's a normal part of life.

How did you feel when you made the mistake? Maybe it was something like this:

I was so embarrassed and ashamed! I won't do that again.

I'm glad I made the mistake because I can learn from it.

One of these feelings comes from a fixed mindset and one comes from a growth mindset. Can you guess which is which?

People who are using a fixed mindset think that their intelligence is fixed. They don't like making mistakes because they think that mistakes mean they are a failure.

People who use a growth mindset understand that the brain is always growing and your intelligence can change. They know that **making mistakes** is a good way to learn.

Let's look inside the brain to understand how making mistakes makes your brain stronger.

Your brain contains billions of **neurons** that pass information to each other. Not all of your neurons are connected when you are born, but as you learn more things, you create new connections between them. This makes your brain stronger and more powerful.

Making mistakes is one way of creating **new connections** and growing your mind power, so don't be afraid to take risks and get things wrong! This book has all sorts of fun ways to help you learn how to develop a growth mindset and learn from your mistakes.

So let's get started!

Feeling down

Some people feel disappointed or ashamed when they **make mistakes**. It's normal to feel that way, but you mustn't let the negative feelings get you down.

Be kind to yourself when you make a mistake. Talk to yourself in the same way that you talk to other people. Give yourself a **brain hug** by focusing on your good bits and giving yourself compliments.

Being mean to yourself about mistakes stops your brain from growing strong. Think of your brain as a blow-up ball. When you think negative thoughts, the ball deflates and the hard times can't bounce away. Thinking positively inflates the ball so that it can bounce away difficult moments.

Riya

I used to love painting. One day, I was working on a new painting of a horse and it came out all wrong. I felt so embarrassed.

I thought I was good at painting, so what had happened? I knew I could start again, but I didn't want to. I was worried that the new painting would be bad as well.

Then, my friend came over and looked at my painting. He said nice things about the colours and the way the horse was moving. I realised that I had been so busy looking at the bits I didn't like that I hadn't noticed any of the good parts.

The next day, I started a new painting of a horse, using the same colours and movement, but changing some bits that I didn't like from the first painting. It turned out really well!

THINK AGAIN

One way of being kind to ourselves when we **make a mistake** is to focus on the fact that we are learning, not failing!

Mistakes are steps on the path to success. A mistake can show us that an idea isn't correct, so we know we have to look for another solution.

Think about walking through a maze. When we reach a dead end, we turn around and try a different direction. Finding the dead ends helps us to find the way out and solve the maze.

All of the mistakes that you make create new connections between neurons (see page 5) in your brain, which boosts your brain power! Try this activity to help you remember this.

On a piece of paper, write down a mistake that you made recently and how it made you feel.

Crumple the paper into a ball, getting out any frustration that you feel about the mistake.

Then, uncrumple the paper and trace along the folded lines with coloured pencils. These lines represent the new connections made in your brain by **making the mistake.**

Keep the piece of paper somewhere where you can see it. When you see it, it will remind you of how mistakes help your brain to connect neurons and get stronger.

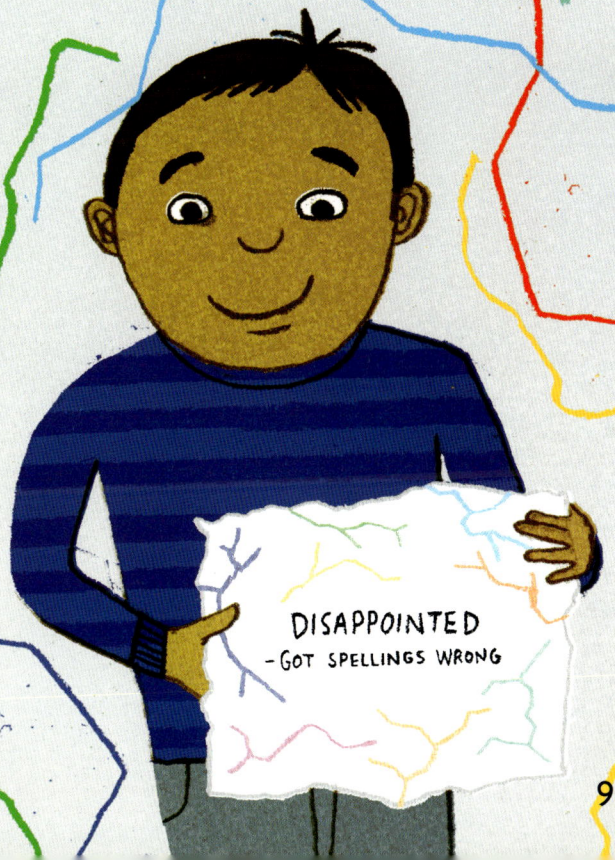

DISAPPOINTED
- GOT SPELLINGS WRONG

Types of mistake ✗ !

To learn from a mistake, it's useful to think about what type of mistake it is. We can sort mistakes into different categories.

A slip-up – made because you were careless or not paying attention

A blackout – made because you forgot or didn't know important information

A misread mistake – made because you didn't read the question properly

An active mistake – made because you chose the wrong approach

For example, name the eight planets in the solar system.

Saturn

Uranus

Mars

Venus

Jupiter

can't remember (?)

Earth

Mercury

Which type of mistake has been made?*

We can use different strategies to avoid different types of mistake.

To avoid slip-ups, leave a few minutes at the end to go through your work. Read it aloud and see if you spot any obvious mistakes.

To avoid blackouts, you might need to study in a different way to help you remember information (see pages 12–13). If you don't know or understand the information, ask for help! Asking for help is a sign that you **want to get better,** not a weakness.

To avoid misread mistakes, take the time to read the question carefully. It can help to underline the important words to make sure you focus on them.

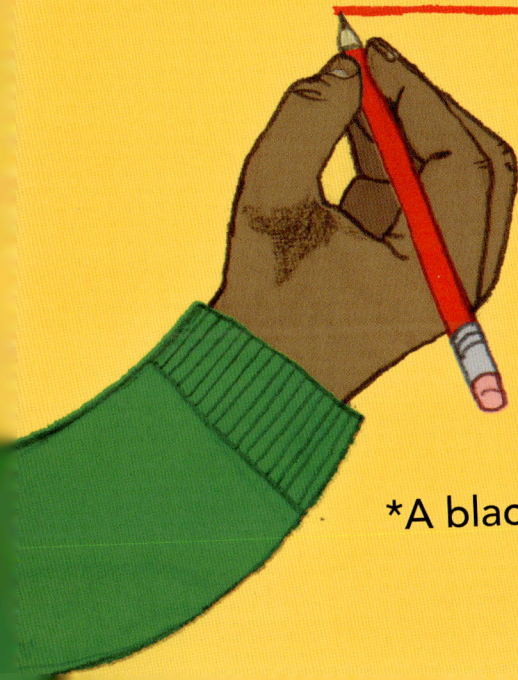

To avoid active mistakes, you may need more information about the right approach or you may need to read the question more carefully so that you choose the right approach.

*A blackout

11

A new strategy

Repetition is important when learning something new. Even if you understand it the first time, it will slip out of your mind unless you go back to it several times.

This is because studying what you've learned makes the connections between the neurons stronger so that the information sticks in your mind.

Sometimes mistakes are a sign that you aren't studying in a way that suits your brain.

Everyone's brain is different, and can change over time. One day, writing things down might help you to remember. Other times, talking might help things to stick in your mind.

How do you study
when you have to learn
something new?

Try some of these other study techniques
and see how they work for you:

★ **Make flashcards.**

★ **Give a presentation to someone who doesn't know anything about the subject.**

★ **Divide the information up into bullet points where each bullet point is a different piece of information.**

★ **Draw a mind map with all of the information that you can remember. Then look back at your notes and add anything that you have missed.**

★ **Throw a ball back and forth between you and a friend. Each time you catch the ball, say something that you remember about the topic.**

A-ha!

Sometimes mistakes are surprises. Have you ever thought you understood something until a mistake showed you otherwise?

This can be a shock, but think of it as an **a-ha** moment instead of a failure. **Trial and error** helps our brain make new connections so that we can find the correct solution.

Think of it as a bunch of keys. Sometimes, you might have to try more than once before you find the one that fits and opens the door.

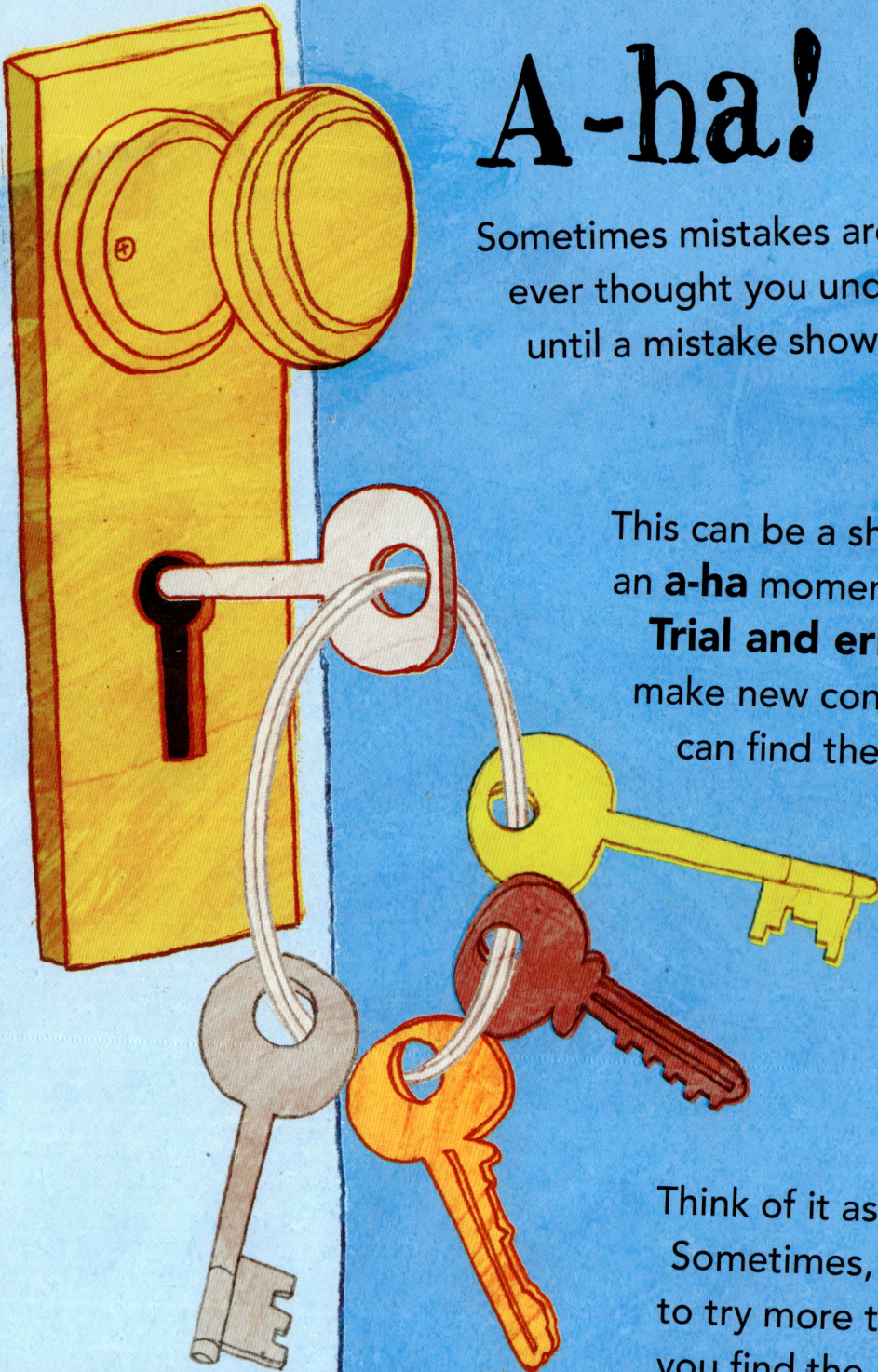

Jamie

Last week, we were taking it in turns
to read a story aloud in class. When it was my turn
to read, I noticed a word in my sentence that I wasn't sure
how to pronounce – **'epitome'**

I'd seen it written down before and I knew it was something to
do with being the best example of something,
but I wasn't sure how to say it.

I gave it my best shot and said it how I thought it was pronounced –
'ep-i-tome'. A few people in the class started to
giggle and I knew I'd said it wrong! My teacher explained
that it was actually pronounced **'ep-i-ta-mee'**

I felt silly in the moment, but then I noticed that lots of
people were making mistakes when it was their turn
and learning how to pronounce words they'd
never heard said aloud before.
Now I know how to say **epitome**
and I won't forget!

A healthy brain

Sometimes we make careless mistakes. We might know the answer, but forget it because we aren't concentrating properly. This can happen when we aren't taking good care of our brains and our bodies.

Careless mistakes don't help your brain grow so you should try to avoid them.

Here are some ways to keep your brain and body healthy:

★ **Eat a balanced diet so that your body has everything it needs to work well.**

★ **Eat regularly so that your brain is powered up to learn.**

★ **Get enough sleep so that your brain can rest and repower for the next day.**

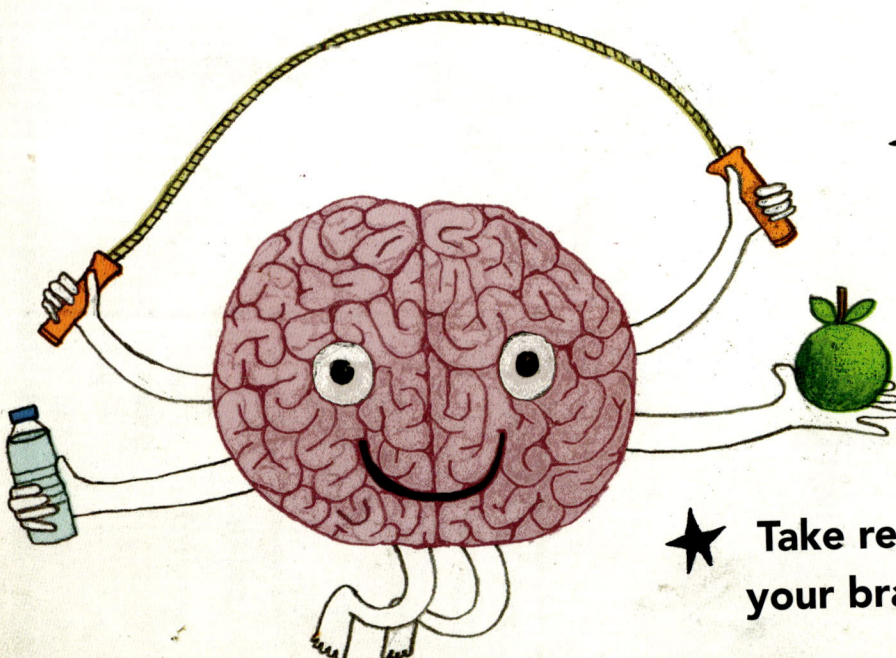

★ **Drink around five glasses of water a day so that your body is well hydrated.**

★ **Take regular breaks so that your brain doesn't get tired.**

Oliver

At lunchtime, I never used to eat all of my lunch.
I was too busy playing with my friends!

After lunch, I normally have science as the last lesson of the day.
It's one of my favourite subjects, but I would always get questions
wrong and forget what we'd learned the day before.

One day, it was raining so we couldn't go outside to play. I ate my whole
lunch, sitting and chatting with my friends.

That afternoon, my science lesson went so much better!
I worked really hard and understood everything.
I could even remember things later!

Now I eat my lunch before I go out to play so that
my brain has energy for the afternoon and I can
work hard in science class.

Time to shine

When you are on your **learning journey**, it doesn't matter if you make mistakes. In fact, you should make them as it helps your brain to grow!

However, there are times when it would be a shame to make a mistake. It could be an important exam, a play or performance, or a sports match.

These aren't learning experiences – they are times to show off everything we know. It would be disappointing not to perform at our best and show off how much effort we have put in.

The best way to prepare for these moments is to go over any mistakes that you have made before.

Go through this checklist:

★

Do you need any extra information? If so, what is it?

★

What have you done wrong previously that you could do differently this time?

★

**How are you preparing?
Does this method work well for you?**

★

Is your brain well rested and healthy before the big day?

If things don't go to plan during the big event, don't be hard on yourself. Focus on what you can learn from the mistakes for next time.

TRYING NEW THINGS

Being afraid of making mistakes can make you afraid to **try new things.** You might think that if you end up making a mistake, it would be a sign that you can't ever be good at it.

But that's not true! **Everyone makes mistakes** when they try new things and these mistakes help us to learn.

Are there any activities that you've always wanted to do but have been afraid to try? Find a time to give them a go and see if you like them. Be prepared to make mistakes as your brain changes and learns how to do the new activity.

Adwoa

I'd always wanted to go to dance class.
Some of my friends went and it looked like so much fun!
But I'd never gone because my friends are such good dancers.
I thought I'd never be able to keep up with them and
I'd make so many mistakes.

Then, last week, there was an open day at the dance school.
My friends convinced me to go along, so I did,
even though I felt scared I would mess up.

I did a trial class with lots of other beginners and I had so much fun!
I did make some mistakes, but so did everyone else around me.

I'm going to keep going to classes and working hard so that I
can catch up with my friends one day! Now, we practise their
routines together, even though it's hard for me to keep up.

Dancing is so much fun, I feel silly for
waiting so long to give it a try!

DON'T GIVE UP

Sometimes when we make mistakes, it can make us scared to try hard and **make an effort.**

We feel like we aren't making any progress, **so why bother?** You might feel like trying and failing is worse than not trying at all.

We can't let mistakes scare us away from trying, as **learning requires effort.** The hard work that you put in during the learning journey makes your brain stronger and helps to develop your skills.

Think about a personal goal that you worked really hard on. Choose something that makes you feel proud.

How did you achieve it?

What mistakes did you make?

What challenges did you face?

How did you overcome them?

How did you feel when you found it difficult? What did you do?

Write down your answers and keep them safe somewhere. Now choose a new goal that you want to work towards. When the going gets tough, look back at your answers for inspiration!

Make the goal specific, as this makes it easier to work towards. For example, 'enter a photo I'm proud of in a photography competition', rather than 'get better at photography'.

Challenge o'clock

As we know, **making mistakes** is one of the best ways to learn new things. Instead of going for safe, easy activities, we need to look for new challenges where we will definitely make mistakes.

Pushing yourself to do hard things is the best way to grow your brain. Just as in sports, your muscles have to work hard (and sometimes feel tired and sore) to grow stronger. It's the same with the brain!

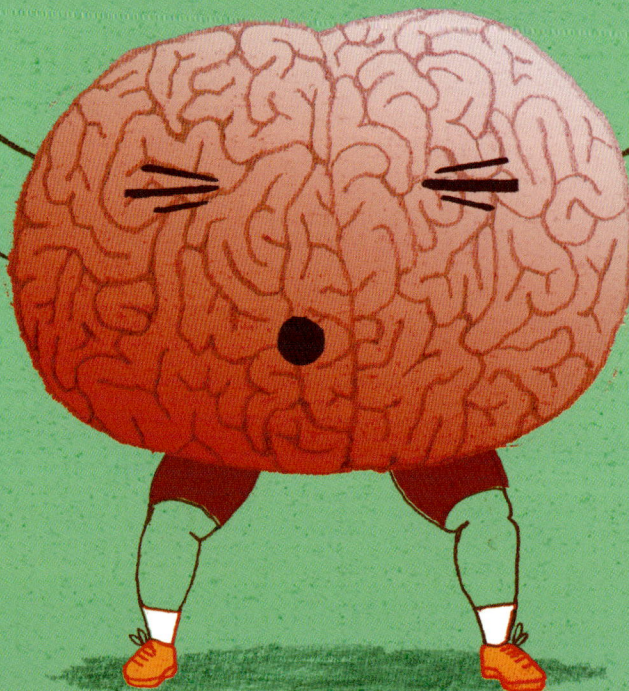

Antonio

Last term, we could choose between two language classes at school – Spanish or Mandarin Chinese. My mum is Spanish so we speak Spanish at home.

I thought about doing Spanish because all my friends were going to do it. I knew the work would be easy and I'd be the best in the class!

But then I thought about it and I realised it would be a waste of time to take Spanish, because I already know it! It would be so cool to learn Chinese, so I chose that instead.

It's hard work in class, and it took me a while to learn how to pronounce the different sounds. But I can already count to ten and talk about my family! I can't wait to learn more next term.

MY BEST MISTAKE

Looking back on past mistakes is a great way to learn for the future – **they always teach us something.**

We can also learn lots from other people's mistakes. Sharing our mistakes shouldn't be something that we feel embarrassed about.

While you eat lunch with your friends at school, or dinner with your family, why not discuss the mistakes that you made today and what you learned from them. Decide as a group who made **the best mistake** and why!

It could be someone who pushed themselves really far. Or it could be someone who put in lots of effort and finally found a solution after trying lots of different options and making lots of mistakes!

You will always remember some mistakes, but there may be others that you forget over time. Why not turn a notebook into a **mistake journal** to track your best mistakes?

In the journal, write down mistakes that you have made and what you learned as a result. It could be new information, such as that the capital of the USA isn't New York, it's Washington D.C.

Or, it could be something that you learned about yourself. For example, you don't do well on your maths homework when you do it while you watch TV, so you should do it somewhere quieter.

You could write in your journal every day or just save it for the really big mistakes that you don't want to forget.

Look back through the journal from time to time and **congratulate yourself** on all of the new things that you learned!

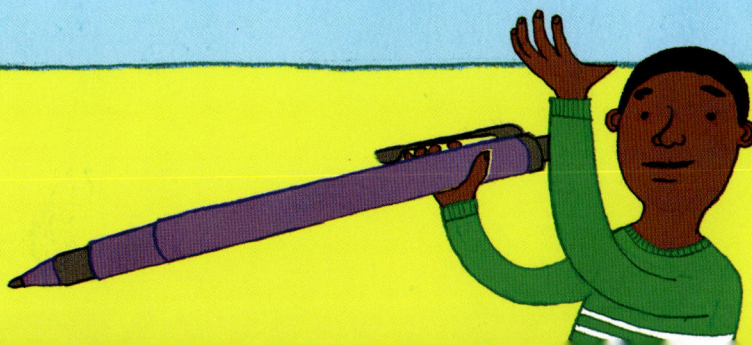

Famous failures

It's easy to think that famous people were born successful, but that's not the case.

Lots of people who went on to experience success did so as a result of hard work, and because they made **a lot of mistakes.**

Their mistakes motivated them to work harder, look at things differently and keep going!

Life is a bit like the game of **snakes and ladders.** You will always encounter obstacles and mistakes on your path that set you back, but you have to keep on going to win!

Research a famous person that you look up to. It could be a business person, a musician, a sports person or a politician. What was their path to success? Which obstacles did they overcome?

Turn your research into a poster. Hang the poster on your bedroom wall as a reminder that we all have to overcome obstacles and fail on the path to success.

You could also talk to your teacher and ask if you could do this activity at school. You could hang the posters in your classroom to motivate others.

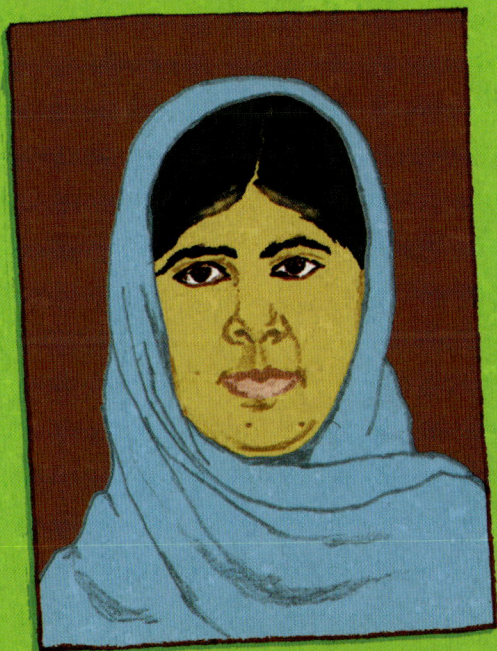

Keep MAKING MISTAKES!

Read through this book's tips any time you need a quick reminder!

Don't be afraid to take risks and get things wrong.

It's normal to feel down when you **make a mistake**, but don't beat yourself up about it.

Remember that making mistakes helps to create **new connections** in your brain.

Thinking about the type of mistakes that you make can be useful.

Asking for help is not a weakness. If you don't understand, talk to your teacher, a friend or an adult.

Studying in different ways can help us to **avoid mistakes.**

Healthy brains and **bodies** are less likely to make careless mistakes.

Avoid mistakes at important events by planning first.

Don't let mistakes scare you away from trying, as learning requires effort.

You can't learn unless you **challenge yourself**, and new challenges often mean mistakes.

Don't be ashamed of your mistakes – share them with others.

Writing down your mistakes can **help you learn** from them.

Get inspired by famous people who have made lots of mistakes on the path to success.

Notes for parents and teachers

The concept of a **'growth mindset'** was developed by psychologist Carol Dweck, and is used to describe a way in which effective learners view themselves as being on a constant journey to develop their intelligence. This is supported by studies showing how our brains continue to develop through our lives, rather than intelligence and ability being static.

Responding with a growth mindset means being eager to learn more, and seeing that making mistakes and getting feedback about how to improve are important parts of that journey.

A growth mindset is at one end of a continuum, and learners move between this and a 'fixed mindset' – which is based on the belief that you're either smart or you're not.

A fixed mindset is unhelpful because it can make learners feel they need to 'prove' rather than develop their intelligence. They may avoid challenges, not wanting to risk failing at anything, and this reluctance to make mistakes – and learn from them – can negatively affect the learning process.

Help children develop a growth mindset by:

- Giving specific positive feedback on their learning efforts, such as 'Well done, you've been practising …' rather than non-specific praise such as 'Good effort' or comments such as 'Clever girl/boy!' that can encourage fixed-mindset thinking.

- Sharing times when you have had to persevere learning something new, and what helped you succeed.

- Encouraging them to keep a learning journal, where they can explore what they learn from new challenges and experiences.

- Inspiring them to take risks, make mistakes and reflect on lessons learned by sharing personal experiences and anecdotes.

Glossary

fixed mindset   if you are using a fixed mindset, you believe that your intelligence is fixed and can't be changed

growth mindset   if you are using a growth mindset, you believe that your intelligence is always changing because your brain can grow stronger

mind map   a diagram with lines and circles connecting different ideas

neuron   a nerve cell

obstacle   something that makes it difficult for you to do something

progress   developing and improving your skills or knowledge

strategy   a plan that you use to achieve something

trial and error   trying different things until you find one that works

Index

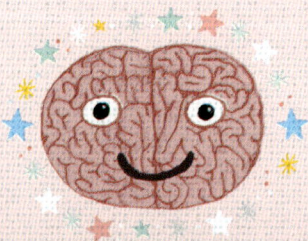

GROW YOUR MIND

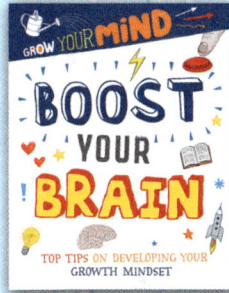

BOOST YOUR BRAIN
TOP TIPS ON DEVELOPING YOUR GROWTH MINDSET
978 1 4451 6860 9
978 1 4451 6861 6

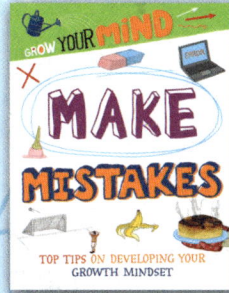

MAKE MISTAKES
TOP TIPS ON DEVELOPING YOUR GROWTH MINDSET
978 1 4451 6923 1
978 1 4451 6924 8

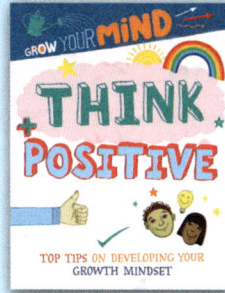

THINK POSITIVE
TOP TIPS ON DEVELOPING YOUR GROWTH MINDSET
978 1 4451 6925 5
978 1 4451 6926 2

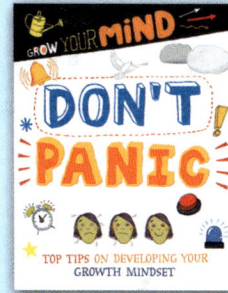

DON'T PANIC
TOP TIPS ON DEVELOPING YOUR GROWTH MINDSET
978 1 4451 6927 9
978 1 4451 6928 6

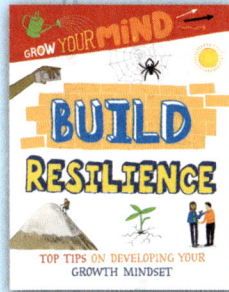

BUILD RESILIENCE
TOP TIPS ON DEVELOPING YOUR GROWTH MINDSET
978 1 4451 6930 9
978 1 4451 6929 3

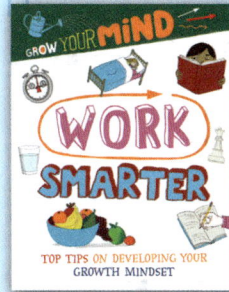

WORK SMARTER
TOP TIPS ON DEVELOPING YOUR GROWTH MINDSET
978 1 4451 6931 6
978 1 4451 6932 3

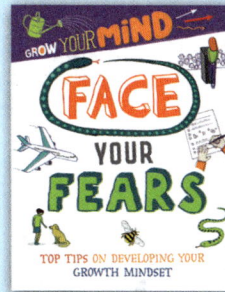

FACE YOUR FEARS
TOP TIPS ON DEVELOPING YOUR GROWTH MINDSET
978 1 4451 6933 0
978 1 4451 6934 7

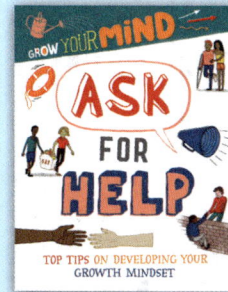

ASK FOR HELP
TOP TIPS ON DEVELOPING YOUR GROWTH MINDSET
978 1 4451 6935 4
978 1 4451 6936 1

Series contents

Boost Your Brain
- A brain-boosting mindset
- Sshhhhhh...
- One thing at a time
- Think, rest, repeat
- Brain hugs
- Time out
- Take care of your body
- Brain dump
- Picture this
- Sum it up
- Make a mnemonic
- Study buddies
- Brainy book

Think Positive
- A positive mindset
- Half-full or half-empty
- All or nothing
- Celebrate
- Thanks for everything
- Smile!
- Truly positive
- Let it go
- Feelings detective
- Seeing the future
- Positive people
- Doing good
- Be kind to yourself

Build Resilience
- A resilient mindset
- The power of 'yet'
- Effort thermometer
- Digging deeper
- Halfway there
- Try to fail
- Positive practice
- Stronger together
- Change for good
- Seeing the future
- Ups and downs
- Rest and recover
- Get creative

Face Your Fears
- Fear and mindsets
- What are you afraid of?
- Meet your fears
- You're not alone
- Being brave
- Little steps
- Big leaps
- Now isn't then
- Story time's over!
- Give it a minute
- See the other side
- Energy swap
- A year from today

Make Mistakes
- Mistakes and mindsets
- Feeling down
- Think again
- Types of mistake
- A new strategy
- A-ha!
- A healthy brain
- Time to shine
- Trying new things
- Don't give up
- Challenge o'clock
- My best mistake
- Famous failures

Don't Panic
- A calm mindset
- Future friend
- Nervous or excited?
- Trust yourself
- Not a competition
- Panic button
- Reach out
- Everything changes
- Do your research
- What can I do?
- What could go wrong?
- If it does go 'wrong'
- Tomorrow is another day

Work Smarter
- Mindsets at work
- Fighting fit
- Get chunking!
- Give it your all
- Activate your brain
- Just right
- Give your brain a chance
- Keep repeating
- Nobody's perfect
- How do they do it?
- Know yourself
- Work smart, play smart
- Be the teacher!

Ask For Help
- Help and mindsets
- Everyone needs help
- Be brave
- Speaking up
- No stupid questions
- Who can help?
- Helping others
- Team power
- Taking feedback
- Sharing opinions
- Working through challenges
- Reaching out
- Helping yourself

W
FRANKLIN WATTS